WHAT ELSE,

BESIDES THE SEX,

is

important?!

VOLUME 1

WHAT ELSE,

BESIDES THE SEX,

is

important?!

VOLUME 1

By
Marcell

What Else Book Publishing
Pittsburgh, Pennsylvania

WHAT ELSE, BESIDES THE SEX, is important
Published by:
What Else Book Publishing
Pittsburgh, Pennsylvania

Marcell, Publisher & Editorial Director
QualityPress.info, Book Packager

TABLE OF CONTENTS

PREFACE

Even though modern life-style centers about fewer marriages, we can assume that modern-day sex-indulgence has become more widespread than ever.

Questioneer:

Mr. Author, what prompts you to believe this?

The Author:

No previous era has ever socially sanctioned <u>the wearing of ladies' dresses</u>...so short.

Questioneer:

Mr. Author, are you saying that short dresses are causing a sexual revolution?

The Author:

Maybe, and when you consider other social-givings contributing elements...increased acceptance of sex outside of traditional heterosexual monogamous relationships (marriage), like the "pill" (free sex), contraceptives, public nudity, normalization of homosexuality, alternative forms of sexuality, legalization of abortion, sex-toys, nonfiction sex manuals, explicit sex on screen, and pornographic materials... the rate of child-birth and abortion will rise... the rate of child-birth to teenagers should also rise... the rate of low-birth-weight babies should soar! These 'givings' imply a greater Sexual Revolution than any previously experienced.

Questioneer:

Mr. Author, where are your facts? The world needs facts, not supposition.

The Author:

I am writing a book . . . of pleasure. I don't have the facts which you request. And I don't need your facts to write this book...of pleasure...so I leave the facts to the readers (or people like you...census experts) to supply. Now, may I proceed...without further interruption?

Questioneer:

Oh, al-right...but it better be good!

Having lived during the 20th Century, and having experienced the world's 'first acknowledged' sexual revolution, every adult should be left wondering "...what else, besides sex, is important?"

Let me offer a few suggestions. People of mercy must pursue helping others. People of pride must prove their dominance by competing against others. People of low-esteem experience being shy, and eager to follow where others may take them, while mildly accepting the humility of being victimized. People of might enjoy forcing their will upon others.

This book **"What Else, Besides Sex, Is Important?!"** will describe which 'roles' the author played during his time, although the author truly believes that every generation has experienced a sexual revolution... since the famous degree... 20 centuries ago... 'multiply and replenish the earth'.

I offer this book to all persons open to enlightenment, who may welcome a few moments of silent excitement ... or confirmation of feelings that all humans will share.

Marcell

Marcell

WHAT ELSE, BESIDES THE SEX, is important?!

HUMBLE BEGINNINGS

As a living creature, recently born (miracle — Stan's body, at birth, was exceedingly tiny and frail. too fragile to survive),

my first recall of intense interest was looking at the sky. Lying in a homemade baby crib, I could look through holes in the ceiling of our four-room house and see the sky. I studied the fascination of cloud formations with various shades of blending colors ... for hours. When it rained, my crib was moved into a shadowy-darkened corner, to protect me from falling raindrops, where I could see nothing... for hours. I wondered what was so important to my care-givers that I was left unattended for such long spans of time, but I'm sure they were into something good. Besides, I'm basically OK. No pain. I'm not 'wet'...nor hungry. I'm really not hard to please ...but the pain I did have, was mental and exasperating. The agony and anxious moments which I suffered, waiting patiently, and desperately wanting to get out of that dark-forsaken corner...while eagerly anticipating the sky to return, again, or to see anything of interest ...made me realize I'm upset, and my blood pressure must be rising out of control.

I promised myself "When I grow-up..."

My family moved away from the Monongahela-River-Bank; and entered another Pittsburgh-suburb, offering signs of real civilization...cobble-stone streets, flourishing small businesses, lighted streets, churches, and schools. I was highly impressed, until the family's next move...again in the same suburb, but living on a dirt street, two blocks from the Youghiogheny River (on one side) and one block from the railroad tracks (on the other side). My thoughts became confused; my values became questioned. "We left one river-area along the Monongahela, to live close to another (the Youghiogheny); We left a cobble-stone street, to live on a dirt road; We are now victims of long and uncertain travel-delays, caused by lengthy slow-moving trains...carrying freight; we are unavoidably exposed to their sustained deafening whistles...announcing their approach; and further challenged to avoid life-threatening dangers presented by fast-moving passenger-carrying-trains ... with no intent to stop. Other inconveniences are noteworthy, but...are we moving-up? Or what?"

"When I grow up..."

This concern disappeared after I was admitted into public school, because my life-style (living near the river...on a dirt road) became quite exciting and exceedingly rewarding. The dirt road (seldom used by vehicles) provided sufficient space for a neighborhood play-ground, and my 'gang' thought it was a perfect arena for daily after-school-football-games. Until the Stantons' arrival, the neighborhood children could only maintain 2-man teams. If I played, the numbers would warrant 4-man teams...at least. No one ever picked me to play on his team. I was so young; my body was tiny and fragile; but I learned how to convert the daily newspaper into a football...which the gang liked'...it's durable with a nice grip'.

During that era, the common expression of acceptability was 'nice'. The weather was nice; the cake tasted nice; sex was nice; everything was nice...so when I heard that my man-made-paper-football had a nice-throwing-grip, I immediately understood that the gang had officially accepted me, not only as a 'gang member'...but also as a football player! As a result of keeping a supply of footballs on-hand, I was always "picked". Always picked last...but always picked.

My problem was to replace the Stanton house supply of toilet tissue, the 'daily newspaper'.

The older boys in the gang mentored the younger members in matters of importance "Lay wid-a girl...ev'ry chance y' ounce git (all heads in hearing distance turned simultaneously with that of the mentor's...towards the Storage Shed)...and don't let out-a-towners mess wid-our (3rd Ward) girls."

The storage shed, a gigantic building...without windows or doors, was positioned near the end of our dirt road, beyond any living quarters, and used to store city vehicles and equipment of bulk size. It had no interior lighting or heat, and its entrance was a huge-barn-like-opening. Everyone in the neighborhood had probably looked-in 'the storage shed'...if only thru curiosity. To me, the storage shed was a place of mystery. During "day hours" it was always whatever it was meant to be, but it usually exuded a mild, somewhat exciting, un-mistakable tangy odor... after dark.

The city "dump" lay 2-blocks beyond the storage house. The "dump", another building of tremendous size, was the city's garbage-disposal-agency. City garbage was received and burned in-doors, then moved to an out-door area (to cool), and later transferred elsewhere...beyond our neighborhood.

This agency, city-garbage, became my 1st source of income.

After school, instead of running with the gang (who preferred walking-girls home, or something else), my daily routine became

Hop a freight...a block from school,

Ride a few blocks...then off you jump,

Change your clothes, and find the wagon,

Then rush off again...to the **dump junk pile**

I piddled through the burnings, searching for metal

Looking for tin, copper, or gold

I needed these assets...swapped for rent

Swapped for money...from the junk-yard-man

The metals I found were always stashed-away before the gang assembled for football, and even later (after supper) I would find time to return to the dump, sneak in-doors, and steal a couple of empty "pop bottles", also, for future recycling-refundable-income. The **"dump"** not only provided my financial needs for daily newspapers and 'comic books', but also supplied me with much needed rent contributions. Returning home, passing by the store house, I filled my nostrils with that exciting, mysterious pungent odor.

Mother Stanton knew this was the last day of 3rd ward public schools before the summer vacation, so I handed my Report Card to her as I entered the kitchen. My mother was normally called 'mum' by everyone, except Dad. Mum, "short & plump", with an unusually quick smile...stood fumbling around with something in the sink. She looked at me, showing a wide, warm smile…but never stopped fumbling with something in the sink. Mum was well past 60 years of age, and had not experienced much-else except poor health, hardships, and poverty…but was seemingly always prepared to generate a pleasant, reassuring image. Her smile painted a higher level of radiance or a new level of joy to an existing surrounding environment. My mother had a gentle, sincere persona. When not in pain….suffering shortness of breath (asthma), or physical discomfort, her facial expression usually acknowledged joy, relief, gratitude, and was one-heart-beat away from an oncoming smile. Her smile lightened the room, and I knew she was truly pleased…with something. I wanted to show my approval of her joy, so I stretched upwards, on "tip-toe", to kiss her cheek. Mum apparently read my mind…turned towards me…held my head between her hands…and kissed my lips.

"Congratulations! I know you passed".

HUMBLE #2

My 2nd oldest sister, Anna, was seated at the tiny kitchen table "shellin' peas" and was so close to the sink area, that she intercepted my Report Card, which I had offered to Mother Stanton.

"All A's, again...excellent behavior, again. Mum, Stan has passed into Jr High School, to the 7th Grade!"

As Anna continued to talk, she reached for some silverware and then approached the stove. I immediately recognized the aroma of warm bread pudding...my favorite dessert...before dinner! I didn't have to ask. I knew that Anna was preparing a slice of bread pudding, for me. My juices began to churn, my mouth was already salivating. I sat down on a makeshift bench...leaned back against a wall...and nervously awaited the go-signal.

While eating, and listening to Anna, I concluded this surprise was 'nice'...better than Xmas eve, when **ALL CHILDREN** are rewarded with pleasantries. This surprise rewards only me, but why? Because I made good grades? Because I give rent? What does it matter...I like it.

Anna continued, "Mum, Stan and Myron (Anna's oldest son) are practically the same age…they live like brothers…eat the same food…get the same up-bringin'. But they are so **different**. I'm afraid Myron won't pass this term. His grades haven't been good at all. I 'spect Stan will catch-up with him."

"Anna", mum interrupted…obviously reading my mind again as she added another slice of bread pudding onto my plate, served with a small bowl of ice-cream…before dinner, "These two boys remind me of you and your sister Tonie (Tonie was also married…with a family). You are full-grown and settled; Tonie has some growing-up to do. She is right-smart, but Tonie is easy to be influenced and she's too quick in saying 'yes'. She must learn to say NO sometimes, and she likes 'the street life'. You do too, but Tonie lives there." While mum spoke, Anna cautioned me, "Slow down. Stop gulping food."

I thought Anna was reminding me of Anton's eating-advice…to chew each mouthful 25 times. Anton is our brother, under Tonie, I said, "Yes mam", but I question the wisdom in referring to bread pudding and ice-cream as being "chew'able foods". Besides, it's getting late. Football hour is near. If I want more surprises, like this, I should continue doing things that made it happen…change clothes wagon…**dump junk pile**.

Anna was right. Before leaving the school grounds, I found Myron Wentel with Don Jacks (Tonie's youngest son) and looked at their Report Cards. I have caught-up with both.

My brother, Anton, 20 years my senior…was one of the single greatest influences of my youth. Because I was born with such a tiny, fragile body…not expected to live; and my father, always traveling, found only meager means to support a family of seven, Anton became a **high-school-drop-out** to join the work-force…and he further assumed complete responsibility for my financial needs. He researched 'blood building foods' and always had these items on-hand…in quantity ... for my personal diet. He influenced my first **charge account**. When mum, or any adult advised me to get a haircut, I said "Yes'm" and I went…even if I had been given no money. I became a client of 3 different barber shops in the 3rd Ward. No barber ever asked me for money; I never offered to pay any barber. On one occasion, I admitted not having any money and the barber said, "I know…Get in the chair!"

During my elementary school years, our dirt road was given a layer of coal cinders…probably to provide greater traction for vehicles traveling over snow-covered roads. These cinders did not off-set the football-hour. As spring approached, during such an occasion, I fell to the ground…my hands absorbed the shock…and cinders caused a 3-4-inch cut around the flesh of my left-hand thumb. Before I could get upset or frightened, looking at blood flowing for the first time, I suddenly realized that Anton was here…out of nowhere…like Superman…had lifted me into his arms, and commenced to rush downtown for medical help. As blood dripped or fell, I was more concerned with the speed at which we were moving. Anton's normal walking-pace was 'real fast'. I had to run…now and then…to keep up with his normal walking-pace. While carrying me, he has exceeded his normal pace, so I assumed Anton was running, but there was no **up-and down** motion. I glanced down at his feet…Anton is still walking! Before I could resolve this confusion, we had arrived at some destination; my hand was treated; and we went home. As we walked home…racing, now and then…I became confronted with another puzzle. Would my bandaged hand warrant 'family sympathy'? Enough to justify my 2^d-favorite-dessert…a chocolate layered cake?

As years passed, Anton bought his clothing and a matching unit (in "boy size") for me. I wondered 'Has he also learned to read my mind?' I had never told him how handsome I thought he was…that I really respect his judgement…that I would want to look (and become) **JUST LIKE HIM**. He supplied me with white-rayon dress shirts…just like his. I also wondered what people were saying about us as big Anton and 'little Anton' always went to the downtown movie on Friday, after school … both wearing a white shirt with neck-tie…one, sometimes running to stay abreast…the other, just stepping along.

As close as the Stanton brothers had bonded in their 3rd Ward address, their love and devotion would surely be tested…and un-done, in their next 1400 3rd Ward home.

HUMBLE #3

As I became more obsessed in the 'daily routine', increased rent contributions, receiving good reports from school, eating properly, and keeping a low profile (staying out-of-trouble...socially), which probably pleased Anton, he sponsored activity which commanded fatherly love from me...for him. I learned to expect and welcome his voice "Wash yourself and change clothes. We're going out." Without any prior notice, I could soon be on my way to a movie, or a professional ball-game, or to the Zoo, or the circus, etc.

During these 'outings', I found little opportunity to volunteer conversation. I didn't know anything to talk about, but I did wonder why we were always alone...why Myron or the Jacks brothers never traveled with us? I loved them as brothers, but I wouldn't dare ask, for fear of implying I was dissatisfied with something which I truly found suspenseful, exciting, and pleasing. Maybe Anton did not want to reward youngsters who were constantly <u>on-punishment</u>.

Anton tried to mentor me in every conceivable eventuality...especially, the worthlessness of females. I had overheard family conversations, which described Anton to be a victim of both love and war; having been shell-shocked during World War Il; then returning home...to find his fiancé married to someone else, so I was not surprised to hear him explain that ladies were self-serving, manipulative, dishonest, not trustworthy and incapable of truth, etc. If the 'family gossip' was true, Anton might have had due cause to feel ugly towards ladies. I have seen my sisters exemplify his thinking...but I knew that **ALL** ladies are not evil-minded. Our mother is not the type he described. On the other hand, Mum might have evil-done my father...somewhere, at some time...while treating me like a king. I believe that would be a sin. Having "favorites" (being prejudiced) is not right, but doesn't everyone have "favorites" (prejudices)? I don't know if she did...or didn't. Everything is possible. I don't know enough about these things to even think about it. This is Anton's problem...not mine. I'm too young for this. Need more "schooling".

After years of reflection I now understand why I did not have a 'favorite academic-class' while attending elementary school. I excelled in all classes and my self-esteem soared. Becoming rated-ISt in the class (valedictorian) was an impossibility of no importance to me, but I felt compelled to be listed among the **honor roll** students. This rating also brought rewards...outside of family.

Students, who had no interest to earn good grades, usually turned their focus to other things. Daydreaming...throwing spit-balls...making fun of someone executing an ugly deed, to get attention. A favorite 'ugly', for boys, was to pull the hair of a girl seated in-front. There was purpose in this madness. Even though the boy, involved, knew he might be reported and punished for committing the 'ugly', his purpose was to show the girl that he would risk embarrassment and punishment...for her affection. If you consider, further, that the girl does not report or complain of his 'ugly' deed, then his purpose has been achieved...without any punishment; and even further, that failure to complain of such 'ugly deed' might possibly invite or encourage **such repetition**, etc.

Stan could not risk being reported for **poor behavior** and in his persistence to earn another excellent rating, he accidentally dropped his pencil...which fell to the floor...introducing to him, a new world.

I was disappointed that my reflexes were not fast enough to catch the pencil which had bounced slightly-backward, on my right side. Leaning down...to retrieve the pencil, my peripheral vision recognized a deliberate motion of-exposure...behind my seat. Martha, seated behind me, had shifted her body to the right side of her seat...with her legs spread apart...allowing me to see her white "panties". After picking-up the pencil, I looked backward. Martha was smiling, and blushing; I was oddly excited. In some strange sense, I thought Martha's smile was reassuring and very important...and I wanted to experience that odd excitement again.

It happened often. If Martha touched my neck, I knew how to react. If I coughed (twice)...and leaned, she knew to perform more so, as time passed...without panties. The view always paralyzed me momentarily. My body quivered slightly. As I looked, I felt powerful with a sense of urgency. The odd excitement had an overwhelming growing presence with an internal swelling-up effect...making me suspect "There's something wrong with my body!"

The cloak-room incident, occurring the following week, satisfied and resolved my suspect. Even though I wanted to 'peek', and Martha would make it possible, I always went home after-school and made no attempt to socialize with Martha. I learned, in the cloak-room, that this odd excitement was normal...and would return, often.

"Recess" was our (out-door) supervised-recreation class, the 1pm afternoon class following Lunch. Many students rushed through Lunch (in the cafeteria) to enjoy extended Recess activity. This was my plan, after I finished my lunch, but I decided to place some comic books upon my classroom-desk before they became damaged or wrinkled during recess-activities. As I dropped the books upon my desk, I heard sounds of movement coming from the 'cloak room'...a closed-in area behind the teacher's desk; a long and narrow space...used to store hats, coats, boots, umbrellas, etc. The cloak-room door was open, so I looked in. Martha stood near the entrance, putting something into her sweater pocket. I said "Hi" and turned to leave.

"Wait." Martha reached for my hand, and pulled me in a suggestive manner. Her touch was soft, inviting, and demanding. I couldn't resist approaching her. As I entered the cloak room, Martha retreated further into the cloak room until her back-side leaned against the wall. Pulling me closer...and even closer...Martha gave me a pecker-type-kiss while she directed my left hand (held within hers), to rest momentarily, upon her stomach. Martha winched, slightly...at my touch and immediately squeezed my hand lovingly, which calmed my concern. I felt her body-weight shift as she spread both feet a-bit further apart, guiding my hand...slowly, under her dress...until my hand touched her leg. Martha winced again. Instinctively, my bent fingers relaxed such that my open palm was caressing and massaging her upper inner thigh. Such smoothness...such softness...no panties. As soon as I realized Martha had relinquished control of my hand, she again reached for my index finger and pulled it upward...further...upward...then, to and fro...very slow...to and fro...very slow. My finger became moist...and penetrated within...each push generated more moisture. and deeper penetration. more moisture...deeper penetration. Martha's hips commenced to sway; she has increased the amount of pressure guiding my finger such that I now have two fingers within!

I liked this, and the odd-excitement is back...more powerful than ever...and growing stronger...and stiffer. But, something is wrong. My trousers are too tight! I can't go to recess, like this...I can't go to class, either...I can't even go home...until I find trousers that fit, loose. And what is this wetness? It must be blood. I don't think I cut my hand...again! Maybe the hole my finger dug in her body is bleeding. Martha does not look like she's hurting. Besides, she's the one who made my finger dig the hole. Where's the blood coming from? How long have we been in here? What's coming next? I tried to withdraw.

Martha, anticipating the withdrawal, suppressed it with such strength that I found three fingers...within.

Later, as Stan re-joined his Recreation-Activity class, he pondered several issues: "How'd she know that I was planning to 'come-out'? Did she make that noise in the cloak-room...on purpose? Was I manipulated? Could I get 5 fingers, or a fist...in there? What made Martha flinch? Why does my body swell-up?...and then shrink?" As he wiped his hand with a handkerchief, Stan resolved another mystery. The 'wetness' was not blood; it had a clear color, and his left-hand fingers have the same unmistakable, pungent odor ... as the storage-shed.

I've learned...that rewards will come if you make good grades in school; or pay rent; or make "nice" footballs. What should I call the 'schooling' I learned...today?

Martha is a big part of that 'schooling'. She may not be a teacher, but she is special...some-how. Because of her, I know there is something in school which is more fun than recess.

And she only spoke one word...wait!

HUMBLE #4

Stan had learned, in Jr Hi School, to memorize part-singing instructions given to elementary classes; and he searched for a method to reproduce the different voice-lines on his living-room-piano by hit-and-miss. When the adults recognized the noise would eventually produce familiar tunes, Silent Night...Twinkle Twinkle Little Star...etc., it became obvious that 'genius' Stan should be given piano lessons...then violin lessons...then baritone...trumpet, etc..

Stan was fascinated with comic books, so he usually kept a few in his school desk, with intent to make pencil sketches of special heroes. It was during one of these sketching experiences that Ms Hall, his home-room teacher, took notice, became impressed, and suggested that he remain after school to sketch a life-sized Santa Claus "bust" on the classroom black-board.

This was achieved with such pleasing likeness that other teachers made similar requests...a sleigh with gifts within...Santa riding on Rudolph's back...Santa, Gifts, Sleigh & Reindeer...sketches, the size of a full blackboard; double blackboard; or total wall.

Stan, already an Honor Roll student, would now reach Celebrity Status, which he might enjoy repeatedly (especially financially) with every seasonal and national-school-holiday.

As the Jacks brothers and Myron Wentel became increasingly delinquent in school matters, and periodical contributors towards a growing police record.... Stan's honor-roll school record, coupled with a clean police record, gave him a "most reliable" type reputation...among family, and community. As a result, the three nephews could only pursue football activities, swimming pool events, or local birthday parties, etc."...**if, and only if** Stan is a participant, or in attendance."

The decision caused my ego to **SOAR**, and the nephews knew this ruling was meant to limit their social activities, but everyone was happy. Whereas the nephews knew that I was doing naughty things...like them, stealing ‹pop bottles' and comic books, or playing sex-games with young girls, etc.... I was never "caught"...nor publicly accused, thus keeping an honest and innocent reputation. They also knew that I wanted to be with them, constantly, and that I could easily be coaxed, or bribed into their advantage.

Because my nephews and I lived in the same house, we were usually seen together as a group, always fighting...whether we were fighting each other, or fighting boys who felt we were invading their "turf" to date their girls, or fighting boys who were on our "turf"; we became labeled as "those Stantons" by adults in the neighborhood, showing their disapproval...but the local young girls were obviously impressed. Seldom did we fail to receive birthday-party-invitations...which occurred often, whether hosted by girls, or boys.

Because we Stantons were well-liked and quite popular, we often conferred with each other to avoid sexual approaches with the same girl. We Stantons had established special protocol for birthday parties, of our age-group.

Each Stanton was certain to acquire sufficient funds to buy an adequate birthday gift, for both, the child and his parents; complete bathing preparations at a designated time on party-day; wear fresh-laundered clothes, and to protect each other's love-interest...at the party.

The hosting-parents were usually very visible as guests arrived, receiving birthday-gifts and strategically placing the gifts in some chosen area; and later, unwrapping and putting the same gifts on display.

The hosting-parents remained visible while serving refreshments to all guests; dispensing with paper plates, or food-serving items; and in so doing, also using a harsh tone-of-voice or negative-body-language to indicate their level of limited...unforgiving...punishing attitude toward unaccepted **social behavior.**

When the parents were satisfied that all guests were sufficiently enlightened of 'proper social behavior', sufficiently nourished (with refreshments), that all gifts were properly received and recognized, and that complete silence was broken only at the sound of their voices...only then, would hosting parents leave the party area, and remain isolated from we-children, with the understanding that the birthday-child would now determine party games or other ensuing activities.

While the parents were receiving and positioning in-coming-birthday-gifts, all guests put on their 'best conduct' face, and the accepted code-of-behavior became...

"don't smile (loud),

don't look (long),

and don't move (wrong)."

As the parents opened gifts, all guests, so fearful of losing forth-coming "fun", forced their best behavior...and were hardly moving, or breathing. Refreshments consumed considerable time; and the guests began to strain with restraint...just patiently waiting, hurriedly eating, nervously sitting, and afraid to cough, so fearful of being singled-out.

When the door closed behind the parents, leaving the party area, the guests experienced a moment of complete silence . . which immediately erupted into a loud simultaneous sigh of relief...as all children knew, finally, that sheer fun and pleasure were just moments away...that they, no longer, had to hold their breath...that only 2 games would be chosen...that 'Spin The Bottle' (a kiss-on-the-cheek-game would only last about 3 minutes), giving way to **"POST OFFICE"**, a 'favorite' for all lovers!

Post Office: A chance to hug a girl, in the dark; a chance to hold or kiss a girl, as often, as long, as she allows; a chance to kiss a girl, without interruption!

The birthday-child would choose a guest to be the Mail Man, who simply stands at the entrance of an empty room (or clothes closet, or any completely private or secluded area), and call a specific individual to come forward to pick-up his mail, stored in the adjacent empty room...without any electric lights.

The birthday-child becomes the first 'sender', positioned within the empty room, giving a specific name to the Mail Man...to be called-forth to receive birthday-child's letters. The person invited into the Mail Room, receives mail (hugs, kisses, etc.) from one person; then remains in the Mail Room…alone, to become the 'sender' (giver) to another.

If any Stanton failed to be 'called-forth' over a reasonable length of time, the other Stantons were prepared to use their control plan … calling-forth only **Stanton-girl-friends**, which would not only get him involved eventually, but might also change the game into a boring "8-person-kissing-rotation" with 4 Stantons & their girl-friends.

Leaving any birthday party, we Stantons would measure our total evening's pleasure, based upon lip-stick smears on our face and handkerchiefs. I measured the degree of my total pleasure... based on "How many of my fingers, of both hands, had the storage-shed's-exotic-&-pungent-odor?"

LOOKING UP

The Stanton home was constantly patronized with visitors, both men and women, coming and leaving, such that certain persons (visiting with such regularity) would eventually surpass being considered merely 'visitor' but more-so as 'honorary family'...without any specific reason for being there. The atmosphere within the Stanton home was usually pleasant, jovial and full of activity. Family card-games could quickly convert into community play...or both. Since Mum and Anna, both, played the piano (quite well), singing...or dancing...could easily consume an entire evening. "Love Songs" were popular; all ladies provided different 'harmony'.

"I was fascinated with family-night; when Mum smiled, shaking her big hips...**everybody danced!!**"

When the Stantons moved away from their 1300 address and into their 1400 (3rd Ward) home, they experienced a huge step-up.

"We lost our **cinder-covered-play-ground**, but we gained a concrete sidewalk. I lost **freight-train transportation** to and from school, but the profit I gained from frequent black-board sketchings (now, at the high school level), had long replaced my need to be near the dump-junk-pile. The family acquired a more convenient bus accessibility, just beyond our front porch; the indoor-toilet (on the 2nd floor) replaced a basement-facility, providing greater comfort and tremendous convenience...our 2nd indoor facility was located within the basement apartment, usually rented-out. Even though the 3 families were still badly cramped, other conditions were vastly improved.

"Annie was a steady-visitor, either <u>arriving-with</u> or <u>to-see-one-of-my-sisters</u>. Annie, in her early 20's, was very attractive and possessed a 'bubbly' personality when Anton was around, but morose...saddened...or conservative, during Anton's absence. Annie wanted Anton, who refused to return her interest. During one such visit, not finding Anton at-home, Annie decided to leave. I had been playing the piano, but decided to quit playing, and then seek recreation outside. As Annie and I met, leaving the house simultaneously, she suggested

'Walk me home?'"...

"'OK," (I was going that way, anyhow. We walked far, and not much was spoken, but when she reached for my hand, I knew that I would soon learn why I was walking-her-home. Annie ushered me into an alley-way; we stopped walking; she wiggled slightly, and her panties were lowered to the ground. As she stepped-out, I admired her beautifully shaped legs. (Annie finally spoke.)"

"Be still." Leaning forward, she unzipped my trousers sat down, showing her exposed nakedness...then lay back, totally flat.

"From the moment Annie reached for my trouser-zipper, I was totally concerned with '...**who is passing-by this alley-**

way (from both directions), **in broad daylight!**' I tried to remember...**what forced me to the ground?...and how did I also fall upon her...without hurting her?...HOW DID 1 GET WITHIN HER?** Suddenly, these things didn't matter. I liked it. This is good. <u>**Real good!**</u> **Better than ANY favorite dessert!!** But what is it? Am I pushing...or is she doing the pushing?"

Without any warning, a compelling force had to be reckoned-with.

"I had to urinate...but not <u>in</u> her."

Stan withdrew, jumped to his feet, and became very surprised. His urine did not 'spray'...it squirted. It had also changed...in color, <u>and</u> texture.

"Annie (now, also on her feet) knew that I had just experienced my first ejaculation (hugged me and gave me a reassuring kiss); also knew that I was embarrassed (rested her lower torso against my 'trunk', and smothered my face with tender kisses); explained 'what happened' to be very normal (as her lower body torso massaged my growing 'trunk'); and she promised more moments like this (the massaging continued...with deliberate stroking...rhythmic stroking); her conversation stopped (as she forced her tongue into my mouth, instinctively seeking, finding and kissing my tongue)."

"...if you like."

Annie was breathing "heavy"; kissing Stan's face, then his tongue. Her lower torso was inter-locked with his; her body 'wiggled'...slowly...to and-fro...side-to-side...up-and down ...round-and-round; sometimes stroking the already-stiffened "trunk". As the stroking-place found its niche (up-and-down), the stroking pace gradually quickened (with greater intensity). Up, and down...up, and down...up, then down...up, then down. Annie's embrace became tightened and very demanding: her head swayed...her arms squeezed...her hands clutched, but the "stroke" remained the same...up, then down...up, then down...up up up up ...! Every stroke brought heightened passion; each "niche", elevated its intensity; each repetition reached for recognition, such that **one** regulated niche-stroke...so firm...so prominent...so constant...so powerful...so intensified, would inevitably cause Annie's lips "to kiss" **everywhere**...her hands "to grip" with **viciousness**...her arms "to grasp" with **greater squeeze** ...**SIMULTANEOUSLY!**

Suddenly, Annie's neck stiffened, momentarily; and her head slumped lifelessly and rested upon Stan's shoulder. Her entire body was in a state of complete rest.

"I was 'out-of-breath', too. Annie was too exhausted to talk, but 'what little' she did say...was really a boost to my ego. I pondered **how powerful I felt.** Even, out-of-breath, I wanted more 'touching'. I also pondered...**what kept Annie from falling down...as she wiggled?...could she balance herself, and still wiggle? was it my strength that kept her balanced?**

I pondered further, if I can find this much pleasure with Annie during broad daylight hours, what can I anticipate...behind closed doors?

My confidence soared, again; somehow, I knew that I had just passed...another test.

During on-coming months, I continued giving adequate time to school work and music lessons, but all leisure hours were spent with Annie. I had become obsessed, wanting to share...and anxious to relive, the awareness of her exposed flesh, which Annie was so eager and willing to share.

"When I finish growing up"...

REACHING HIGHER

" A nnie's influence re-arranged my list of priorities. No more football games after school; no more hanging-out with the gang; no more birthday parties or participating in family activity during evening hours... I wanted Annie. I preferred to be with Annie, at her place, where 'touching' was plentiful...incessant...and uninterrupted. Self-committed, I simply learned to crave **Annie,** and her sweetness. Annie, and her softness. Annie, and her encouraging....inviting smile.

My thoughts always followed her; my nostrils, always searched for her perfume; just thinking of Annie, **my Annie**, brings such excitement that the 'oncoming anticipation' would cause my 'trunk' to harden.

Annie and I never attended church services together, never went to the local Movie Theater...nor any other public activity. She did not ask to be 'courted'; I did not 'suggest' moving-into her place, nor to pay rent; but I was perfectly content to lounge-about at her place as long as she availed herself. We had one thing in-common. 'Touching.' And we indulged constantly. Annie was such a cheerful giver! She encouraged my sexual suggestions, initiating sexual activities so I became quite comfortable playing the sexual-aggressor-role. She felt complemented that I would find her 'sensuous' in such a variety of circumstances.

After the blissful passing of many months, I realized our age-disparity had never been discussed; nor had our **relationship-commitment** ever been defined, but our 'touching' blossomed, such that Annie became 'forever bubbly', knowing that I would return...again, and again; and I grew into greater confidence...quite aggressive in showing love, and inducing sex, also knowing that Annie would respond, not only willfully, but adequately...to any such aggression.

Word came to me, while at school, that a girl (3 or 4 grade levels below me) had boy-friend thoughts of me. Having obsessed-like affection for Annie, I ignored this information. However, fate caused us to cross-paths often enough that I noticed '...**she may be too young, but her body is the right size."'**

Long, shapely legs; two breasts...perfectly matched, both "proportional & equilateral", appearing like 2 oranges pushing outward...to avoid the confinement of a moderately-tight-fitting-blouse. The small of her back reminded Stan of a ski slope. A <u>beautifully-rounded</u> ski slope. Stan thought...'**I'd love to see those apples...without restraint!'**

"Fate must have known that I was destined to lose Annie; that Annie would eventually move out-of-the-state; that she would only return...as a married woman.

"As I rushed into the local **Theater,** I had no thoughts of Annie; nor the youngster'; nor any girl. I came to this theater with the excitement of hearing (once again) **'Wild Bill'**, boasting 'I'm a peaceable man'...and then pistol-shoot 3 or 4 bad men, after knocking-out 2 or 3 bandits with his bare hands...still wearing his two-gallon-hat. The main feature **THE WOLF MAN** had already begun. Two ladies, seated to my left, drew my attention as they exchanged seats. The 'youngster' was now sitting next to me, in the seat vacated by her cousin...the informant.

"As the wolf suddenly lunged-upon a victim, people in the audience reacted...with screams, etc. (thus, warning the victim of threatening danger); the 'youngster' grabbed my left arm (a female-desperation-gesture-against fear by clinging to her lover for protection); as she clung-and-held, massaging my left arm (my "trunk" began to stiffen); my right-hand stretched, to "cover both of her hands, held firmly to my upper-left-arm (as my left hand drifted under her coat, and rested-upon her leg); the 'youngster' offered no resistance, as she looked at me...and smiled (I released her hands, sending my left hand to browse for hidden treasure ...the warmth and softness of her bare knee, then the upper-inner-thigh); the 'youngster' scooted towards my seat as far as possible...thus resting her head on my shoulder. As my left hand continued to browse, further and closer, the 'youngster' scooted again, **forward,** as she simultaneously repositioned her overcoat (resting in her lap)...not only to hide my left hand completely, but probably, to provide greater convenience and **unlimited freedom** for further browsing...wherever!

"My 'trunk' is as stiff as wood; it wants to stretch further than the trousers will allow. It huffs and burns...like, when I climax, but...I didn't feel the 'squirt', and no moisture...either."

Stan decided to leave. **"Come! We're leaving."** I stood-up...reached for the 'youngster's hand...and we three left the theater.)

Stan evaluated his predicament: "This 'youngster' really impressed me. To be so young, this girl is really smart. Are all girls 'smart', like this? Martha (my age) taught me several things...only speaking one word. Annie would surely know about sex and 'climax'; she's older than me. This 'youngster' has consented to sex...without being asked; even knows about suitable positioning. She must be an expert in <u>what-to-do-before-sex</u>, and better yet...<u>how-to-best-enjoy-sex</u>!"

Stan's mental evaluation continued: "I left the theater because I was no longer-comfortable there, and I had no idea, either, as to what I would do with these girls. However, I had never experienced such sexual excitement; Annie had never forced such physical-attraction upon me. I feel compelled to understand...or, to experience...more...without restraint."

Stan concluded: "Decisions...decisions...decisions."

WOW ... I'M RICH!?

L eaving the theater, Stan could readily envision how he
would spend the next 2 or 3 hours, with the
"youngster"...lying on a rolled-up rug, stored in the basement
of his 1400 address. Stan also understood the wonderful gift
which fate had arranged for him...2 young girls, always
giggling, showing no resistance towards sexual advances,
leaving the theater prematurely...to satisfy the whimsy of a
stiff "trunk"? The "youngster" had her own reasoning for
sharing his excitement.

"He's holding my hand! He's <u>still</u> holding my hand!! I'm
glad he's got a hold-of me. I'm so excited. If he let-go, I'd be
jumping up-and-down. That would be bad. I don't want to
seem over-anxious, but I am! He's so cute. All the girls at
school like him...but <u>he's</u> with me! Out of all the girls at
school, he's with me. He wants **me!**

"His hand is soft, like a girl's; but I feel power in his
touch, far more than a girl's. He's the best piano player in the
whole school; and he **<u>wants me!</u>**"

Stan thought he had mental-control-power over the
"youngster" as long as he held her hand, so he was reluctant to

release it. Stan soon pondered an embarrassing-public-discomfort: an exaggerated, protruding "trunk", within the confines of tight-fitting-trousers. Caressing and squeezing her hand kept the "trunk" fired-up in a ready-to-go mode (quite visible...very noticeable, unfortunately, if 'down-town,' and during broad-daylight). Stan found a solution...stall for time...wait for darkness.

"Already standing in front of a soda-fountain store, I pulled the girls inside; placed our order; and rushed the girls to sit at the nearest public-table (hiding the embarrassing discomfort, but still holding the hand). I gave the 'informant' sufficient money to pay for 3 bowls of assorted ice cream."

The cousin smiled, accepted the money and rushed to the counter to retrieve our orders.

"Because the cousin showed such eagerness to oblige, I knew I had a good plan. Then, I explained to the 'youngster' that we would walk the cousin to any desirable destination; drop-her-off there, to proceed to her home, alone; and then we would both proceed to my place, following a round-about-route to avoid public recognition."

The "youngster" said nothing, but her smile said everything. Stan assumed the glow in her eyes acknowledged her approval; and hoped that her wide-eye facial-expression acknowledged complete trust in his decision-making potential. Stan looked at her lips, and thought

"...**not thick, not thin, no make-up.**" He scanned her face "...**symmetrical features, satin-smooth skin.**" He noticed his aroused "trunk" to stiffen, again, as if the total-Stan-mechanism had just become aware of being the recipient...to "lay" with such unblemished youth; or

30

anticipating the total thrill of sleeping...with such tender un-touched softness.

He also noticed that he no-longer-had-hold-of-her-hand; and even further, still remained, apparently, in control. Stan wanted to kiss her, and wondered if her lips were also primed, hungry, and begging to be kissed.

"Stan Stanton walks past my house every day. I like him. He's different. The Stanton boys have a bad reputation, but Stan is the 'good one'. The high school teachers give him money, for <u>something</u>! He pays his piano-teacher to teach him; then he teaches the rest of the students whatever his teacher taught him. I like him. Everybody likes him; especially, the girls.

"He's not 'stuck-up'; he was elected **President** of a local boy's club; plays street-basketball with his gang, every Wednesday; but his favorite hang-out is the community Pool Room.

"I know all-about him...when he goes to his violin teacher; or the movies. He does not have a girlfriend. I like him.

"Today, the **Wolf Man** was my best friend. He scared me; I grabbed

Stan's arm; now Stan is with me...focused on me...making plans, to take me...someplace...anywhere. On this day, **I will follow**."

As Stan approached the outside-cellar-entrance to the Stanton home, he reminded the "youngster' of his plan "to sneak into the basement". Neither had spoken much, after leaving the "informant". Both had intense-mental-concerns with such possibilities that could off-set his plan...his "touching plan"; possibilities that might circumvent his sex-touching plan; possibilities which would prevent 'his receiving' her precious gifts: exotic pleasures, and the excitement of anticipation...which she has long accumulated, and deeply stored, within her bosom of purity.

He entered the house, un-noticed; walked down the basement steps, un-noticed; un-locked, and pulled the cellar door open; and, now risks, the ONLY REMAINING POSSIBILITY! Did the cellar-door squeak loud enough to attract family curiosity?

"We (standing perfectly still, not moving, hardly breathing) waited a few moments, which seemed an eternity. I knew our thoughts were the same; that we had the same fear. We braced ourselves, prepared to run. Night-fall was to our advantage, to hide our identity, if forced to 'retreat' to our round-about route; but nothing occurred to indicate our presence had been detected.

We, still, found no reason to talk; no need for preliminaries or foreplay; and, finally, no restrictions...or limitations. I kissed her, very gently; and her body trembled, her lips quivered. I felt power surging throughout my body, but I withheld, momentarily, to allow for her resistance...which never came. I tightened my arms around her; kissed her top lip; then her bottom lip; reached under her blouse, with both hands, scanning her bare back (no 'bra'); I reached under her skirt, with both hands. Her lips, like a violin, stayed in the 'vibrato' mode...a long time."

INVESTMENT YEARS

Stan accepted Annie's absence with the "youngster's" emergence. Although Annie had inspired and cultivated his masculine-identity, Stan now pursues greater enticement...the untouched virgin. He is now convinced that his obsession, then...and now, remains Sex primarily **(not Annie)**, with two prerequisites; **attractive physical and willingness to engage.** Whereas Annie, always available, had no rivals, Stan now understands that he must not wholly-depend upon the "youngster", with limited availability, to satisfy his heavy-sexual-appetite.

"I must 'play-the-field'; get other girl-friends."

Whereas Annie's place had always been immediately accessible, Stan pondered,

"I must search-for local homes which provide transitory-rented-rooms."

Stan's first priority was <u>to increase his income</u>! His current income could not afford 'rented rooms' very often...and he would want several, often. 'Blackboard sketchings' had well-satisfied his financial needs, as a boy; but

Annie's absence has made Stan realize, his boy-days are gone. Stan is now doing man-things:

(1) sex…2, 3, 4, 5 times each week

(miracle — Stan escorted girls into empty homes, seeking shelter for sex …without harm, nor police arrests, nor discovery)

(2) making rent-payments at home (3) making monthly Xmas-Saving-Club payments {for college tuition} (4) "…am I too young to provide my own personal expenses…hair-cut, clothes, shoes, etc.?"

(miracle [lost] — Stan's Guardian Angel allowed him to enjoy his God-given gift "controlling-the outcome-of nocturnal-dreams"…until the gift became 'useful monetary gain')

Anton became a drop-out, from high school, to help support family needs. A 'brilliant mind' became reduced to manual-labor…during times when jobs were few. He spent his latter years in gambling-dens. Whether self-taught, or professionally trained…he accumulated well. His dresser drawer was fastened-shut, with both…a 'combination' lock, and pad-lock-and-key. Few others, if any, had ever been privileged (or authorized) to view (or remove) such contents: mounds, and layers of paper money (of all denominations), scattered loosely…so thick and loosely scattered, that the top layers of bills totally-hid such contents…underneath: several pairs of dice [craps], many decks of cards {Bicycle [both Red and Black]}, artist type-paint brushes, and paints [of different size and color], assorted instruction-books, magnifying-lens, etc.

"My father did not go beyond grade ll in the public-school system, but he spoke the English language wonderfully-well, far beyond that which his formal training suggests. My father was a legitimate automobile mechanic and a genius with electrical appliances; but was equally handicapped...without capital, nor education.

"His 'best-loved-skill', was shooting Pocket Billiards. My father was so good, he could make the balls 'dance'. His peers refused to play him; so, he traveled to make a living, playing against others, who could make the balls 'sing-and-dance'. Whenever Dad returned-home, visiting, I lived in the pool room; usually crowded with men...also anxious to witness the exhibition...of dancing balls.

"Dad contracted sickness; became hospitalized; and was transferred from one institution-to-another, for years. Anton was always close, reacting or responding, to the needs of Mum, Dad, and me.

"Dad was a handsome man of small stature; always clean-shaven, with a professional appearance. He usually wore a 'suit', when indoors; but always wore a hat, when outdoors. Dad was equally articulate with social graces.

"Missy (Mum), why don't you use silverware to eat your soup? You look dumb and stupid...drinking soup in a bowl."

"Mum (typically not wearing her dentures), finished drinking and chewing such vegetables within, stood-up, wiped her lips with her left wrist, then placed that left wrist on her left hip, turned (facing Dad), and finally spoke...defiantly."

"Listen to me, Mister-High-and-Mighty-Richard. If I choose to look **dumb and stupid**, that's my business! **Not yours!** I'm grown...free...white...and way-past-twenty-one. And I do as I damn-well-please. And any son s-a-bitch, who only went to the second grade and don't like it, can catch a bus...and go right-on to hell!"

"Dad, not threatened of her words, noticed Mum (taking deep breaths, face turning red, with hand no longer on her hip) inching closer towards her favorite cooking-skillet, then decided to leave his lunch...unfinished, not to risk any eventuality...greater than a temper-tantrum, reached for his hat, and left. I heard him mutter ..."

"dummy."

Stan followed his father to the pool room, gaining amused enlightenment with every stride. He had just witnessed a family quarrel, wherein his mother released frustration over a disappointment which Richard had caused her...somewhere in their "past". Obviously, she forgave-him...then; but the quarrel was simply a reminder, she has not forgotten.

"Even though I seldom saw my father...here and there...off-and-on...when times were good, I was proud of him; had respect for him; I loved him. Anton played the-father-role also...providing my necessities...anticipating my pleasantries...establishing my career...**full-time!** He also offered these things to both Mum and Dad.

"Anton's dresser-drawer would have resolved my financial crisis; but I felt a need to prove myself worthy of his trust. Like Dad, I turned to the pocket billiards; like Dad, my peers refused to play-me; I risked playing against opponents, who were Anton's peers...who possessed greater-developed pool-skills. My natural talent did not compete overwhelmingly, but I did average modest winnings to maintain a monthly increase to the college-fund and home-rent; to ensure a happy week of sex, and rented space; and, periodically, contribute to a new wardrobe."

GREATER INVESTMENTS

S tan's high school years were very productive, especially
with music. He played the 5th-chair-violin in the school
orchestra, which won **'all state honors'** during his senior year;
but really stood alone, traveling with his piano teacher who
presented him in piano-recitals…raising college tuition fees;
and introduced him to local fund-raising clubs, who readily
scheduled such performances: Bach, Brahms, Beethoven,
Chopin, Rachmaninoff, etc.; Stan became a social celebrity.

Local politicians further recognized him; offered him a
summer-job (locker attendant) within the County Park
(swimming pool). During 'slow-time' (inclement weather,
etc.), Stan spent many hours practicing-on-the-piano…stored
within the Barn Dance-Hall.

"Practicing, to perform-well, was important. Practicing
classical music had social significance, also. The noise itself
would attract attention, and also curiosity, bringing visitors.
Most visitors looked-in…then left. Those who
remained…were surely 'unique', and 'persons-of-substance'. If
those who remained were attractive females, they

automatically became a challenge to me...a targeted-priority, in **MY** ball-park."

The gang's **Boy's Club** emerged from a need for more-frequent-birthday parties. The purpose of this group was to provide sexual-opportunities, periodically, each month... within local homes, at certain hours when hosting-parents were at work (out of town, etc.). The gang considered these "pre-arranged-opportunities" to be <u>Club Meetings</u>. Minimal 'dues' were accessed, to later purchase gifts for that household.

"We were called the **Kings**. The girls liked what we were doing; decided to join us...in attaining our 'goals'. We then became...the **Kings and Queens**.

"Attendance increased; dues increased; purpose expanded...greater charitable-effort, sponsoring Community-Bingo. The **Kings and Queens** prospered with ecstatic energy; enhancing my popularity, especially with feminine companionship.

The 'youngster', having never attended the **King and Queen** club meetings, approached Stan..."

"This girl told me that she is your girlfriend!?"

Stan pulled her close, reached under her skirt, found the center of her back, forced his middle finger underneath her panties, slid the finger down her 'crack' until...it found moisture. She kissed him. Her bottom lip quivered ... again.

Stan's piano teacher had forwarded a partial-payment to the college for his freshman semester tuition. Stan would learn, from the registrant's office, how to make full-tuition; and he had already saved $600, which could be used for that purpose.

Anton suggested that Stan should accept the "adoption plan" which his piano teacher has offered, and 'be set for life'.

Stan's parents, knowing they had no financial help for him, refused to influence his decision. Stan did not choose to break one woman's heart (his mother), at the expense of improving another woman's social-status.

"I don't want to break Mum's heart, just to please someone else."

Anton lost his patience

"That's the dumbest thing I ever heard! Nobody could be that stupid! No brother of mine could be that dumb. You couldn't be my brother. I don't **ever** want to see you again."

His words hurt and stayed with Stan…for years, but Stan was so 'hyped' with success, anticipating college-experience, expecting <u>so many</u> good-bye kisses that

"I will abide to his wishes <u>today,</u> but..."

Stan suspected his brotherly-love for Anton was so deep-rooted, and pure…that Anton would not…<u>could not</u> ignore him, forever.

COLLEGE!?

Stan had thought the 700-mile-train-ride to the college-campus-site would be a quick and pleasant experience; that the train-noise would put him to sleep; that he would wake-up and find a reception committee waiting...and singing

"**Hap**-py **days** are **here again**; let's **wel**come **Stan**ton **here** to**day...**"

"Wishful thinking. The train did not put me to sleep; and the rocking rhythm of the moving train, with the constant rumble of its spinning wheels, would only allow me to sing one song:

'**Yank**-ee **doo**-dle **went**...to **town**; & **Rid**-ing on his **po--ny** he **stuck**...

"The 'rocking' continued; the 'rumble' remained; and so did '**Yank**-ee **doo**-dle **went...**'

"I tried to match happy days to fit this rhythm of motion. No such luck! '**Yank**- ee **doo**-dle...

"I knew my problem was 'mental', but I didn't have the resolution. '**Yank**-ee **doo**...

"This <u>just-could-get-serious</u>. I cannot sing this song for 700 miles. **'Yank-ee**...

"My 'Guardian Angel' knew of my predicament, and rushed to my rescue, as two young men walked past my seat looking for a **crap-game**. This expression carried the correct 'tone', and a wonderful melody. I was immediately transposed out of one mental mode; and <u>into</u> another. The 'Yankee...was gone, and the rumble of motion...also. The new mood is, simply, excitement and anticipation."

Stan remembered Anton's counseling

"Never treat dice rough; they'll cause you to 'fold'.

Give dice respect; they'll keep you warm.

The dice will 'come' (win); the dice will go (lose);

Give a little push; you'll always win."

"We found the game in a sleeper-compartment, crowded now, with nearly ten players...some, who had lost, made space for we-new-comers. The bed had been forced out of its original placement, now resting upon a makeshift platform, completely surrounded by the players. Periodically, the players...volunteered to adjust the bedspread, making it tighter...finalizing <u>perfect</u> conditions (for shooting-craps).

"I remembered how to <u>properly-position</u> the dice, before the lifting & shaking; and how to <u>properly-push</u> the dice, before the <u>proper-release</u>."

Stan had won $80 before the game was interrupted, dispersing the players. He pondered:

"That was the easiest-and-quickest money I ever gained. Maybe 'crime' does pay. Is 'gambling', really a crime? Or, is it, more accurately...a 'sin'?

Maybe Anton was right

'...to live the lifestyle which is easiest (more comfortable) for you...no matter who gets hurt or short-changed.'

"Maybe this college will help me to understand these complicated situations, which I continue to run into. And since this college will be my next <u>home</u>, for four (or more) years, I should give it a-fair-shake. So, I here-by forgive the college-people for not showing-up at the train station."

Leaving the Train-Station and approaching a near-by-bus-stop, Stan walked past a local pool-parlor. Knowing that his luggage would be forwarded to the campus, he felt free to squander a little time, browsing-about in the city, just a few miles from the campus; but he failed to realize that his Guardian Angel had to confront restrictions . could not respond to his asking, unconditionally; that he is no-longer a boy; that he must now face consequences...for <u>bad decisions</u>.

"As I entered the pool-parlor, I immediately recognized the 9-ball-game, in progress...typically identified as the 'last table'. I strolled, very slowly, observing each table...knowing my real interest was the 'last table'. The five tables were not <u>all-in-use</u>; and the players (like me) could not make the balls sing **nor** dance; so, I felt comfortable and confident, that my total winnings would surely exceed $80...before I reached the campus.

"I reached the last table just in time to see the 9-ball fall; the loser (a well-dressed young man) throw money on the table; return his cue-stick to the rack; reach for his coat; and leave. The winner (a much-older man), wearing overalls, looked at me...pleadingly

'Wanna play? $1-a-game.'

"I knew this man was not a college-instructor; but he offered me the 'welcome' which I had hoped-for. **Of course**, I would play; and I tried to hide my elated excitement when I responded 'Ok, I have some time…to kill.'"

"Go'n to the college?"

"Yes, this is my first day. Just got-off the train (This fellah might be just a common laborer but he's no 'dummy'. Maybe I should go-easy with him; let him win…a little)."

Stan missed occasionally, on-purpose, but still won each game. The 'farmer' raised the 'ante' (money bet). Stan continued to miss, on purpose, yet continued to win. Stan, very confused … accepted the farmer's suggestion

"You are too good. I can't beat you. Let's play my game! It's quick, and not so tiring."

"What's your game?"

"Three-card-Molly (the farmer reached within an overall-pocket, retrieved a deck of cards, and continued). **I use three cards…any three cards…fold them** (lengthwise) **like this…so all three can hide what's underneath...this** (grain of) **corn. I shuffle the corn...from one-t'another. And when I stop shufflin', you guess where the corn 'tis. If I shuffle slow e'nuff, you win. If you guess wrong, I win."**

As the farmer spoke, Stan thought

"This man is really intelligent...coming-up with a card game which I have never heard-of; a game which Anton had never mentioned. I like this game."

"Ready to start?"

"Yes (this man is 'old'…I am young…his hand-speed can't possibly compare to my young eyes) **Middle!"**

"You win… (the farmer lifted the middle card, showing the grain of corn)"

Stan received his winnings, and further mused: (this 3-card-Molly is easier than shooting craps)

"Middle again."

"You win (lifting the card)**...let's double the 'ante'?"**

"OK ... (1 pointed) **Left."**

      "No (lifting the card), **it's right...I win."**

          "No, I win again."

              "No, I win again."

                  "No, I win again."

After losing more than $680, Stan wondered

"How did it happen?"

Guardian Angel: The farmer out-smarted you. He duped you.

"No! I watched him, closely. He did <u>nothing</u> but shuffle the cards. Besides, I was the one **<u>choosing</u>** the losing-card."

Guardian Angel: You failed to see that he stopped 'shuffling', each time, **<u>exactly</u>** when you blinked your eyes. After each 'blink', the farmer knew that your blind-guess was to his advantage. You guessed correctly...occasionally, here and there; but your blind-guess was consistently wrong. And don't forget, the farmer may have helped you to win...here & there, just as you had planned to help **<u>him</u>**...when playing pool.

"I don't believe that 'old man' did...what I saw him do...time after time...within a blink-of-an-eye!"

Guardian Angel: You admit being a 'young man'; going to college to acquire greater wisdom; so you must also recognize, now, that you have much to learn...especially, about other people and what they can...

"Look here, it's **my** thoughts that are important here. <u>I</u> am the author of this book, so let **me** continue to consider my dilemma. Besides, I just realized a hopeful solution."

The farmer has asked for help, and Stan has consented to assist him...to send money (cash) to the farmer's mother, living in 'parts-of-Georgia'. 'Only-Heaven-Knows' what the farmer saw in Stan...so impressive, that he revealed the contents of his money-belt.

"The farmer had never been 'to school'; could not read-or-write; asked me to look-at the money, which he wanted-mailed to his mother. His 'over-all' was a one-piece-unit, with shoulder straps; his tee-shirt had short sleeves, and an open-neck. Reaching under his tee-shirt, unlocking the belt-strap, he pulled out the money-belt quite easily. Two things caught my attention, immediately. Looking at nothing-but-paper-money, of all denominations, made me think of Anton's dresser-drawer; I admired how-well the single tee-shirt and double shoulder straps had hidden the contents...underneath.

Stan continued to ponder

"I am 700 miles from home; without money; and without friends. I've even turned my Guardian Angel against me. But that can't be! Guardian Angels can't turn against you, because they are on-your-side; they must love you...unconditionally. I've got a plan. It's a good-one! It will work...with, or without...an angel."

Stan convinced the farmer to travel to his dormitory (on campus) to acquire an ink-pen, stationary, envelopes, 'stamps', etc.; that he should only send 'mother' seven-$100-bills (to avoid **suspects** of a heavy letter). As they rode the bus enroute to the campus, Stan, so engrossed and concerned with eventualities that might off-set his 'plan', had very little to say.

The farmer, truly excited, carried the conversation about the joy, and pleasures which the letter would bring. Already totally engrossed, Stan felt compelled to listen to his 'pleasantries', for fear of making a **dumb** statement later...totally destroying the farmer's confidence, and also...ruin 'the plan'.

"Arriving on campus, I found my dormitory (shocked to find such dirty rooms/hallways); my bed; my desk; and my luggage. I unlocked my trunk; found stationary etc.; sat at my desk "What's your mother's name?"

"Matilda Jennings."

"1 addressed the envelope to Stan Stanton...not Matilda. The farmer had found interest, looking out of a distant window. **What is her address and street?"**

"As the farmer dictated the information I asked for. I addressed the letter to my campus PO box."

"Are you Stanton?"

"Turning towards the voice, I faced a young man, **Yes ... I'm Stanton.**" "I'm Skippy, your room-mate. We have a meeting in an hour.".

"Where?"

"Up-stairs, room 201."

"Thanks...**What city does your mother live-in?"**

"You gotta-be Stan Stanton!"

Stan turned to face another room-mate, "**Yes, but how did you know?"**

"To learn anything here, check the bulletin-board. My name is . . . "

"I'll meet you formally...at the meeting. I have something here which I must finish. **Mister Jennings, please bring 'the stuff to me.**"

"Yes, sir Mr. Stanton, here 'tis."

"The envelope rested upon my desk, deliberately, faced-down; I received and spaced 'the stuff to count them; I folded 'the stuff (rather tightly) within a sheet of plain-white typing paper; I reached towards the desk; slid the wrapped-stuff into the open envelope; lifted, moistened and sealed the envelope (still faced-down, away from view). **What's next...Mister Jennings?**"

"We need a stamp."

"I flipped the envelope right-side-up...and immediately flipped it again, to the faced-down position...having clearly recognized the stamp...and the addressed-print, both up-side-down! **No Sir, we need a mail-box.**"

Mr. Jennings followed Stan to the nearest mail-box-unit, outside the dormitory. Mr. Jennings held the chute open; Stan dropped the letter within...still faced-down.

FIRST-YEAR COLLEGE STUDENT — "FRESHMAN" ('DOG') STATUS

"**L**ooking back, I find pride and pleasure attached to my deeds and reputation, while attending college...my first extended-stay, away from home. Reflecting further, I can also refer to bad decisions which brought consequences...

greatly contributing to marital-divorce a few years later, and definitely causing poor health, 50 years later. Hopefully, they, who read this book, will be young enough to avoid these choices...and wise enough to be fore-warned.

**"The tragedy of life is not that it ends so soon,
but that we wait so long to begin it."**

W. M. Lewis

"I never saw the 'farmer' again; I never received the letter; and my Guardian Angel has not made any effort to explain its' failing. Today, I am pleased that 'the stuff never arrived, bringing different consequences...and other unpleasant eventualities...

(miracle — Stan's Guardian Angel must have arranged the letter to be-intercepted; thus releasing Stan from receiving 'the hate & revenge", surely to be generated by the farmer, his mother, etc.... at some later date);

but, at that time...desperation forced me to the **Blood Bank**, often. Honest...but stupid!

(miracle — The Guardian Angel would not permit Stan to fall into poor health...having made too many trips to the Blood Bank)

"Looking back, I can hear my counselor & college-instructors discussing ' Stan Stanton' during staff meetings."

He's a music-major...and he can't sing!

But he's resourceful; created a choir-position (librarian) for himself, to maintain choir membership.

He created another self-position, teaching 'instrumental music'... to the entire community.

He's the only 'dog' on campus, with "teaching credentials".

He plays Chopin...beautifully.

Stan has a student-job in our Printing Department; they speak highly of him.

After 'supper', he disappears.

He spends more time, "off' campus.

He won't be humiliated as a 'dog', with embarrassing-initiation antics.

He is so dignified, he intimidates his upper-classmen.

I hear he's sweet-on Mabel Billings.

He's wasting his time, there; knowing her aunt, Mabel is <u>not</u> putting-out.

Well, I know **Mabel!** If his people had money, he just might <u>ride </u>into-the-sunset.

Stan is a small fellah, but he is no whimp.

Scrappy enough to make I [St]-string college-basketball team, in only 3 weeks of practice…without **any** prior ball-playing experience.

His fragile body won't withstand the rigors of physical competition.

His piano performance was highly praised by visiting VIPs, last month.

"If I had known, <u>then</u>, what I suspect people said about me and Mabel, I would continue (even today) to give her my prime interest, as well as my prime 'pursuit'. Mabel's lips were meant to be kissed; and proved, most rewarding. I learned to kiss every part of her face, neck and chest…anything not covered. Her arms, encircling my neck, and her encouraging smile…demanded 'more'. My kiss caused her body to respond; her upper torso leaned against my 'frontal' so tightly…so closely, that our breathing became in-unison; our tongues, locked within…enjoying the rapture of 'endless-depth'; her lower torso, in writhing, rhythmic movement…with my 'trunk', growing harder…reaching never-known length… ignoring pain…frantically seeking <u>release</u>!

"Going home, I smiled, realizing mixed emotions. Disappointment, yes. I had failed again. Mabel is the first girl who has been able (or smart enough) to withstand my **serious-**

persistent approach, without submitting. Disappointed, but not hopelessly.

"I've tried to touch (kiss) her naked breasts; to get either hand under her dress; but Mabel has been alert enough, not only to anticipate such intent, but to off-set every attempt. However, I can't quit. I **won**'t quit. Sooner or later, I will catch her off-guard, or simply recognize the moment when she's too-weak-to-resist. Besides, other girls…who did submit, have not generated such **memorable-moments**, with the suspense and excitement…which I always find in Mabel. After a day-or-two, I should be strong enough (without Pain) and **<u>dry</u>** enough…to start-all-over."

UPPER-CLASSMAN YEARS

"Mabel remained my greatest extra-curricular interest for three years. I spent most holidays and summer-vacations, at home, searching for 'the youngster', or 'the body', whom I met at the County-Park-Swimming-Pool."

"I'm sorry, I didn't mean to interrupt..."

"Don't apologize; I was really getting tired."

"You are so young, to play...that-kind-of-music."

"**I practice a lot** (her bright, wide eyes danced incessantly...up and down...looking at me...from head-to-toe). **Say, are you here with a group, or are you...**"

"Yes, but the others are swimming."

"Why don't we go to the refreshment stand and get a coke?"

"Whatever you say!"

The substance of her words, coupled with the softness in her voice tonality, confirmed her willingness...and 'suggestive mood'. She was unusually attractive, with a shape which resembled the Coca-Cola bottle. Always smiling, avoiding his eye-contact, she moved (constantly) with a jerky-like effect, or controlled-fidgety, which further accentuated her sensuous appeal. Every movement forced his attention upon some body-part, exquisitely proportional, sensuous, and 'inviting'.

Like 'the youngster', her head stood upright, with pride; her shoulders leaned backwards, emphasizing the beauty of her chest area...and breasts. Stan sensed that she was very young; and quite shy; and that she was desperately searching for a specific or definite-sense-of-direction. **That**...he could give her. First, he would build her self-assurance level; then raise her self-confidence; eventually, give her...total independence. But, "laying" the foundation must come first.

Stan noticed another youngster-quality, small waist (up-front)...sky-slope (to the-rear). As he reached for her hand, Stan's "trunk" stiffened; and he tried to hide his excited-anxiety. Satisfied that she would not resist, he anticipated her "lower torso" to be <u>even softer</u>, and **just** as receptive.

Approaching the refreshment stand, Stan heard her words over-and-over again (**what-ever you say...what-ever you want...what-ever'...**). He remembered a song, which symbolized his thoughts

Row...Row...Row your **Boat! Row...Row...Row** your **Boat!**

'The body' was very impressionable and seemed totally fascinated with Stan. Living locally, she came to the Barn...daily, to avail herself to his asking. Stan welcomed her accessibility and found equal delight with her flexible body...comfortable in any position.

Stan has performed, favorably, for more visiting VIP's than any other graduating-music-major. Is he still the acting-choir-librarian?

Yes, he has passed the **test-of-time**. Especially since he presented 'handprinted-choir-membership-certificates' to the Music Department for each graduating person.

He only has interest in Mabel, music courses, and his night-job; he sleeps-through all other classes.

If you were in college, working all-night, shouldn't you find sleep...somewhere?

I thought he worked in our Printing Department.

He resigned, right after all those **repeated semester-exams,** a couple years back.

I heard he was selling the tests, which **he** printed.

If all this is true, I am really impressed. The young man has resolve. **Wonderful!**

He certainly does have resolve; he refused to sleep with me.

Me, too.

Don't feel bad; he has a 'new love'.

You mean the 'singer' in the choir?

Yes, Melody Brooks...the lyric soprano; one of our finest recruits (1st year student).

Cross her off your list. Stan has her "hooked"...good! She will become a "mother", much quicker, than a singer, for the general public.

"Ma" Green tells me they come 3-times every week, and stay for hours, near dark. She gives them the **Bridal Suite**.

We <u>know</u> what he does <u>there</u>! What's he doing, after supper hours, with Mabel?

We should be discussing Stan's Senior-Student-Piano-Recital. Personally, I think his technique is weak and his repertoire is limited. Stan does not measure-up to our established standards; and cannot qualify for college endorsement.

He plays "Chopin" **better** than others...who **do** qualify, it's true; and I <u>love</u> 'his 'Chopin'; but, can we afford to lower our standards...for any reason? Tomorrow, we'll find a different reason, for a different student; and eventually... there goes our 'reputation' (credibility).

<u>This</u> student, Stan Stanton, suggested and also fulfilled a badly-needed position for our college choir. And he did not 'sell', react-to, or perform <u>anything</u>...without **'our'** endorsement. We authorized him...to **TEACH**...that's what **we** do, and to **<u>REPRESENT</u>** the college...campus as <u>we</u> do. Stan volunteered to teach (the general community), to provide professional print for the Music Department, and we <u>all</u> know what value he has given to this campus...by visiting VIP's.

But...

<u>Pardon me, please! I'm not through!</u> These virtues, of leadership and achievement, are goals which we try to install within <u>all</u> of our students; and Stan revealed these skills...as a 'dog', without receiving **one iota** of criticism or discredit.

As far as Melody is concerned, Stan may have misled or persuaded her…as we have tried with him, but we <u>also</u> know that **he**, quitting the best-and-easiest-student-job on campus…does have resolve.

Maybe, Melody came-on to <u>him</u>! Maybe, we are assuming too much. Melody is still attending classes; and we must wait another year before a child is born. Stan will have graduated before that eventuality comes to pass.

Have you forgotten that he excelled in sports, playing Basketball?

He only went-out for basketball to prove a point. His room-mate called him a 'whimp'! Ironically, Stan's room-mate…a large, well-built, handsome fellah, only qualified for 2nd string-forward. I'm convinced; let's sponsor the recital.

He can't graduate if his tuition is not paid.

Wrong! The statute of limitation is not applicable. Stan can "march', receiving a blank diploma. He will receive his <u>degree</u>…only when his tuition is paid. The recital-date is not contingent upon his graduation date.

A MAN FINALLY

"The college staff must have communed with their Guardian Angel to foresee 'the singer' providing me with a family of 5 children. The 'singer', indeed, was a prized-college-recruit; and the college anticipated wonderful achievements, which she would bring. She would also join the renowned Celestial (college) Choir…without an audition; and being of rigid-religious upbringing, her character would appear…impeccable. Thus, the college would surely welcome the longevity of such talented service which she, obviously, brings to its music department.

Our first glance acknowledged mutual-interest; the touch of her hand (reaching for her music folder) assured me that we were destined to become lovers, that she would not allow religious-concepts to stand between us.

Like **'the youngster'** and **'the body'**, Melody wanted her identity molded within my values. Passion had prevailed **mightily** during my early-teens; and college life provided the opportunity for me to explore and enjoy as much sex as I could digest. Melody and I, were a good-fit, with similar interests…frequency."

After each choir rehearsal, Stan led her to the sex-chamber. "Ma" Green, so accustomed to their frequent visits...their willingness to help-entertain her friends, socially...their exchanging-shopping favors...and so pleased to develop a Mother-Daughter relationship...etc., that she gave Stan a house key; and invited them to the full-use of her home.

It was there, in the Bridal Suite, that Stan spent long hours, giving the 'singer' full benefit of his total sexual-knowledge...without reservation, nor resistance, nor interruption.

"My Guardian Angel had provided various 'jobs' which supported my obsessions.

These gifts (jobs, etc.) correlate with similar gifts which all people possibly receive, I believe, from respective 'Angels'...during the puberty-adolescent stage.

As a man, finally, strongly entrenched in such conviction, I welcomed the challenge to seek more meaningful employment; thus, completing tuition payments and to further support my obsessions, and the needs of my family."

Many years later, Stan retired from the teaching profession; and shortly thereafter, was inducted into his High-School **Alumni Hall of Fame**, brought forth by the following:

He was an accomplished musician

Entertained a diverse clientele:

 multiple social "tea parties"

 multiple VIP receptions (Political/misc.)...

 multiple "memorial" recognitions

 multiple piano recitals

Performing instruments: piano, violin

His wife (a coloratura soprano) & children joined him, creating a "touring ensemble"

He was a dedicated teacher

managed High School band students to become Professional (rock & roll) Entertainers

taught modern-math-concepts (late 50's) before **Modern Math** was published

won 2 Basketball trophies, coaching: **6th Grade Girls**, and **6th Grade Boys**

grade levels taught

multiple years: Elementary, Jr High, Sr High, & College

educational subjects taught...

multiple years:

English/Literature, Reading, Science (elementary), Mathematics (Jr High), Music-Theory, Band (Jr High & Sr High), Orchestra (Jr High & Sr High), and Choir

Teaching Assignments:

Pre-college Math Instructor	1 year
Math Tutor/Coordinator	1 year
Learning Counselor	2 years
Urban Youth Action (UYA) Math Instructor	2 years
Adult Basic Education (ABE) Math Instructor	4 years
GED English] Reading•, GED Math	1 year
GED Math (college-offering)	7 years
GED Math (general population)	2 years

Math/Music Tutor	2 years
Math tutor (Iron Workers)	5 years
Math tutor (Physically Handicapped)	2 years
Math tutor (General population)	3 years
Music (Upward Bound Program)	2 years
Change-Making Skills	1 year
Gate Keeper (College Math Lab)	2 years
Asst Gate Keeper (College Reading Lab)	2 years

Business-ventures

Asst Manager, Coach-House (family) Restaurant	1 year
Manager, Local Fast-Food-Delivery-Service	2 years
Sales Manager (Fire Safety Co)	2 years

Teaching reputation

Implemented an educational career which spanned nearly 50 years

Husband, father, mathematician, teacher, educator, mentor, coach, artist, performer;

consummate motivator, demanding "student involvement";

with a patient, sincere, and encouraging demeanor;

epitomizing qualities of integrity, humility, class, and dignity.

"Dad, thanks for the parenting and teaching you have given me and many others."

PHILOSOPHICAL VENUE

Miracle — At 29 years of age, Stan Stanton's station-wagon (loaded with music equipment & 5 high school band students), slid-off an ice covered hill with no guard rails, while traveling to a weekly "gig". A tremendous-sized (brick) bolder, 5 ft off the highway, deeply entrenched within the earth...prevented the automobile from falling

Miracle — At 50 years of age, having fallen-asleep "at the wheel", Stan awakened to find only 3 car wheels on solid foundation

Miracle — At 79 years of age, still with a tiny & frail body, Stan endured and survived massive heart surgery (double by-pass & valve replacement)...which is, in itself, remarkable

Miracle — 5-Months later, Stan shoveled waist-high-snow for 5 days...without any ill-effects

These latter miracles have forced me to modify my philosophical view concerning Guardian Angels. They (God) will always defend, protect, and guide us...at any age, if we communicate...and especially, if we remain deserving.

SUMMARY

Questioneer:
Mr. Author, you promised to define important elements that all mankind would experience.

The Author:
Did you enjoy reading this book?

Questioneer:
I got a chuckle, here & there; but that's a poor response, for your promise.

The Author:
This book has good length. You could not complete its reading without having memories of childhood-curiosity; or having thoughts of your childhood-dreams; or feeling the anticipation of "completion"; or finding pleasantries which forced you to smile; or accepting fulfillment, when your dreams did materialize; or realizing the excitement involved when you anticipate the repetition of materialized-fulfillment.

So, if you found just <u>one</u> chuckle…I have succeeded in the writing of **PLEASURE**.

Questioneer:
But where are the important features?

The Author:
That, specifically, is an individual-issue. Of individual taste. Personally, I don't find many concerns which I would rate 'more important' than sex; but I did mention those which were more important, to me. <u>Your</u> list, I'm sure, would surely differ from...

Questioneer:
You are **so right, I...**

The Author:
You obviously disagree with much of my thinking. Please tell me, would you read **MY SECOND BOOK**, if 1 should publish a second?

Questioneer:
Yes sir, I would! Especially if you discuss 'fulfillment' and 'dreams', again, like you did in chapter...

CPSIA information can be obtained
at www.ICGtesting.com
Printed in the USA
LVHW052008290120
645201LV00024B/530